MRS
BEETON
SOUPS
& SIDES

Mrs Beeton How to Cook

Mrs Beeton Soups & Sides

Mrs Beeton Fish & Seafood

Mrs Beeton Chicken, Other Birds & Game

Mrs Beeton Classic Meat Dishes

Mrs Beeton Cakes & Bakes

Mrs Beeton Puddings

MRS
BEETON
SOUPS
& SIDES

ISABELLA BEETON
& GERARD BAKER

FOREWORD BY THOMASINA MIERS

For my grandmothers Nora Baker and Elsie Hinch,
who spanned the gap between Isabella and me.

Gerard Baker

This edition published in Great Britain in 2012 by Weidenfeld & Nicolson
Originally published in 2011 by Weidenfeld & Nicolson as part of *Mrs Beeton How to Cook*

1 3 5 7 9 10 8 6 4 2

Text copyright © Weidenfeld & Nicolson 2012
Design and layout copyright © Weidenfeld & Nicolson 2012

Design & Art Direction by Julyan Bayes
Photography by Andrew Hayes-Watkins
Illustration by Bold & Noble. Additional illustration by Carol Kearns
Food Styling by Sammy-Jo Squire
Prop Styling by Giuliana Casarotti
Edited by Zelda Turner

A CIP catalogue record for this book is available from the British Library.
ISBN 978 0 297 86685 5

The Orion Publishing Group's policy is to use papers that are natural, renewable and recyclable products and made from wood grown in sustainable forests. The logging and manufacturing processes are expected to conform to the environmental regulations of the country of origin.

Printed and bound in Spain

Weidenfeld & Nicolson
The Orion Publishing Group Ltd
Orion House
5 Upper St Martin's Lane
London WC2H 9EA

An Hachette UK Company

www.orionbooks.co.uk

CONTENTS

FOREWORD

Although *Beeton's Book of Household Management* came out long enough ago for such chapters as 'Domestic Servants' to be read as social history, her popularity after all this time stems from her straightforward approach to recipes and her beautifully clear detail. Like our beloved Delia, Isabella built her hugely successful career on writing down recipes that actually worked, and were accessible to her readers, making them easy-to-follow and therefore indispensable.

This famous book was designed not just to inspire but also to assist women in the art of 'keeping house'. Whilst such terminology may not curry favour with some brands of feminists today, keeping house is in effect what most women still have to do (as well as juggling everything else), perhaps with far less training than our forebears.

Having cooked for nearly 30 years, I maintain that being able to whip up endless plates of great-tasting food at home relies just as much on keeping your cupboards and fridge cleverly stocked as having a creative flair for food. Yes, you want to cook food that is fun and delicious but to manage this every day of the week requires considerable organisation.

So how does one feed one's family healthily, most nights of the week, under a strict budget whilst still keeping one's marriage sexy and getting the housework done? Mrs Beeton may not have every answer but she does at least give concise, clear instructions on how to cook simple and delicious food that is in season and mostly affordable.

From the simple and everyday – braised red cabbage; five ways to cook potatoes from mash to gratin; mushrooms on toast and a pea soup that is actually the colour of peas – to the more technically challenging (how to make a jellied game stock; wild duck and mushroom broth), this collection gives you classic recipes that you can keep turning to as tried-and-tested friends, happy that they will never let you down. Mrs Beeton does it again.

Thomasina Miers

THE INIMITABLE MRS BEETON

When Isabella Beeton first published *Beeton's Book of Household Management* in 1861, Britain was changing from a rural society, in which large numbers of people were involved in farming and many grew their own fruit and vegetables at home, to an industrialised one, where the development of modern transport networks, refrigeration and kitchen appliances brought a world of food to our fingertips.

Today, most of us have an image of Mrs Beeton as a matronly figure – brisk, efficient and experienced in the kitchen. In fact, Isabella Beeton was young and recently married, juggling working outside the home with running her household and coping with the demands of a husband and young family. Having worked on it throughout her early twenties, she saw her book published at the age of 25 and died just three years later.

Although she wrote of housekeepers, butlers and valets, her semi-detached in Hatch End was a world away from the big country houses of the preceding century, and although it is likely that she had some help in the kitchen, she almost certainly managed her home and most of the cooking herself. Her book was inspired by an awareness of the challenges faced by women like herself – and with that in mind, she used her position as editor of *The Englishwoman's Domestic Magazine* to pull together the best recipes and advice from a wide range of sources.

She was among the first revolutionary food writers to style recipes in the format that we are familiar with today, setting out clear lists of ingredients and details of time taken, average cost and portions produced (this last being entirely her invention). She also offered notes on how to source the best food for her recipes – placing particular emphasis on such old-fashioned (or, in our eyes, surprisingly modern) ideas as the use of seasonal, local produce and the importance of animal welfare.

It is easy to see why Mrs Beeton's core themes – buy well, cook well and eat well – are as relevant today as they were 150 years ago. Her original book was written with an awareness of household economy that we can take lessons from too. Because we have access to so much so easily, we often forget to consider how to get the most out of each ingredient – yet maximising flavour and nutrient value and minimising waste is as relevant in the twenty-first century as it was in 1861.

The right ingredients

Mrs Beeton's original recipes have needed careful adaptation. In some cases, the modern recipes are amalgamations of more than one Beeton recipe or suggestion, which I hope give a more coherent whole. Many of the ingredients that may seem at first glance universal are so different today from those varieties Isabella would have been familiar with that using them in the original way can give quite different results to those intended. For those reasons, quantities needed to be not only converted but checked and altered. And all those cases where Mrs Beeton advised adding salt or sugar or honey or spices 'to taste' have been pinned down in real quantities, always keeping in mind both flavour and authenticity.

Cooking methods, too, were in some cases not replicable and in others simply no longer the best way of achieving the desired results. A significant factor in this is that the domestic oven was in its infancy in 1861, and Mrs Beeton was not able to make full use of it in her book. Most kitchens would instead have been equipped with old-fashioned ranges, and there is much mention of setting things before the fire, turning and basting. Baking or roasting, which we now consider simple processes, required constant attention 150 years ago. Oven temperatures, therefore, have all had to be deduced from a mixture of reading between the lines, comparing modern recipes, and testing, testing, testing.

The end result, however, has been to produce dishes that Mrs Beeton would, hopefully, have been happy to call her own.

The legacy

After Isabella Beeton died early in 1865, her book took on a life of its own. It was endlessly enlarged, modern recipes were added and eventually, in the many, many editions of the book that have been published in the past 150 years, the spirit of the original was lost.

The picture of British food that Isabella painted in the first edition was about to change wholesale, and her book was destined to change with it. The aim of this collection is to reverse those changes: to return to real, wholesome, traditional British food, which Mrs Beeton might be proud to recognise as her own – and to put to rest the matronly image.

INTRODUCTION

The market gardens of inner London that Isabella Beeton knew have almost all disappeared. In fact, the move away from local producers was already underway by the time she published her book of household management in 1861. By the middle of the nineteenth century the railway network had already begun transporting garden produce at greater speed and from further away into London markets. While this brought increased choice, it also created more competition, causing the decline of the inner London market garden.

The majority of vegetables produced in Britain are now delivered directly to supermarket depots and into industrial food-processing units. However, many British cities are still ringed with farms that supply local wholesale vegetable markets on a daily basis. This ensures that the fresh produce found at local greengrocers in such cities is much more likely to be grown locally and brought in on a daily basis.

If you are looking for something unusual, small producers at farmers' markets are often the best source for specialist vegetables and salad crops. There are even some enterprising collectors of wild herbs and leaves, reviving the centuries-old practice of foraging, who will send goods to you by mail order.

Keeping it fresh

Vegetables are an excellent source of nutrients and dietary fibre, making them an essential component of a healthy diet. Eating a mixture of cooked and raw vegetables will ensure you receive a balanced intake of most vitamins and minerals. Once picked, however, the vitamin content of vegetables drops rapidly so, if possible, it is best only to buy what you will need for one or two days at a time.

Even though the nutritional value of vegetables has been understood for many centuries, vitamins were unheard of until the first half of the twentieth century. Cooking vegetables in order to retain their vitamin content was not a concept known to Mrs Beeton or her contemporaries. We now know that some methods of cooking are better than others for preserving the vitamins in vegetables. For example, green vegetables in particular contain water-soluble vitamins such as B and C, which can easily be lost through lengthy boiling. Therefore, some of the modernisation of the recipes in this book has revolved around preserving goodness that might have been lost using the method in the original recipes.

Superior flavour

When a vegetable is harvested it begins to either die or prepare itself for a period of inactive growth, and this alters the flavour. The fresher the vegetable the better the flavour is. In the case of vegetables where the edible part is a storage organ, such as potatoes and onions, the initial sweetness of the freshly picked vegetable immediately alters. Anyone who has ever harvested his or her own vegetables will have noticed how rapidly this change can occur. A freshly picked pea or asparagus spear will taste noticeably less sweet just hours after being picked. Once harvested from the parent plant, they begin to turn any sugars they contain to starch, which is the complex form of carbohydrate that most vegetables produce as they age. Starch can be split into smaller sugar molecules, as when vegetables are cooked at very high temperatures, causing them to brown and caramelise. Grill some asparagus over wood embers and you will experience this to delicious effect.

Year-round availability

Even in Mrs Beeton's time, gardeners were in the habit of forcing fruits into early cropping inside heated greenhouses, or holding back grapes in storage, their cut stems held in charcoal water. Indoor growing is big business today and has extended the seasons of many of our most popular fruits and vegetables significantly. The phrase 'permanent global summertime' has been recently coined to describe the more or less permanent availability of all types of fruit and vegetables in wealthier countries. Approximately 60 per cent of the fruits and vegetables on sale in Britain are imported, either by air or by sea, often from as far away as the southern hemisphere during their summer to see us through our winter.

This raises many issues, but to bring it down to the most personal level, eating in season what is grown locally to you, days rather than weeks after it has been harvested, makes most sense for your health and your pocket. The availability of fresh, locally grown fruits and vegetables can still change rapidly. Some, such as strawberries or asparagus, have a very limited season and it is worth knowing when to expect them.

These pages contain a rough guide to seasonal UK produce and major European crops but, since exact timings can vary with latitude, altitude and local microclimates, it is always worth talking to your local producers and suppliers and asking them which fruits and vegetables will be the next to appear. Tropical crops have not been included as they tend to be available year-round.

Cooking Techniques

When considering how to prepare a vegetable, the cook's first thought should be to maximise the flavour and retain the nutrient value.

Steaming

This is the best technique for cooking vegetables because none of the flavour and very few of the nutrients will be lost during the cooking process. During steaming, ensure that the water is boiling rapidly and turn the vegetables regularly to ensure they cook evenly. A little salt will ensure that green vegetables remain green and bright. Some varieties of potato are best steamed if they are to be mashed or roasted, as they break up less and are drier cooked this way.

Boiling

This technique is commonly used to cook vegetables, and is especially useful when cooking more than your steamer can hold. Salt added to vegetable cooking water will help to maintain the colour of green vegetables in particular. It is best only to boil vegetables briefly in order to retain the maximum flavour and nutrient content. If you are using a large quantity of green vegetables, cook them in small batches and cool them once cooked. Then, reheat in a little butter in a pan and stir over a medium heat to warm them through.

Frying

Frying vegetables in oil or butter is a very rapid way to cook them because the high heat used when frying makes the vegetables brown quickly and easily. Stir-frying in particular is good for retaining colour, flavour, texture and nutrient content.

Braising

This relatively slow method of cooking vegetables using moisture is excellent for roots such as carrots, and onions, red cabbage and dried beans. The flavour of the original vegetable softens and amalgamates more easily with that of the other ingredients, as in the recipe for braised red cabbage (see page 56).

Roasting

Most root and stem vegetables roast beautifully. In almost all cases, partly cooking the vegetables by boiling or steaming them first helps them roast evenly and prevents them going rubbery during the roasting process.

A Seasonal Guide to Vegetables

'To be acquainted with the periods when things are in season', wrote Mrs Beeton, *'is one of the most essential pieces of knowledge which enter into the "Art of Cookery".'* Here is a rough guide to seasonal UK produce and major European crops. Since the crops can vary with latitude, altitude and local microclimates it is always worth talking to your local producers and suppliers and asking them which vegetables will be the next to appear.

January
Vegetables: Beetroot, Brussels sprouts, cabbage, carrots, celeriac, celery, chicory, garlic, horseradish, Jerusalem artichokes, kale, leeks, mushrooms (cultivated), nettles, onions, parsnips, potatoes (maincrop), purple sprouting broccoli, radicchio, radishes, salsify, shallots, swede, turnips

February
Vegetables: Beetroot, Brussels sprouts, cabbage, carrots, cauliflower, celeriac, chicory, garlic, Jerusalem artichokes, kale, leeks, mushrooms (cultivated), nettles, onions, parsnips, potatoes (maincrop), purple sprouting broccoli, radicchio, salsify, shallots, swede, turnips

March
Vegetables: Beetroot, Brussels sprouts, cabbage, carrots, cauliflower, chicory, garlic, jersey royal new potatoes, Jersualem artichokes, kale, leeks, mushrooms (cultivated), nettles, onions, parsnips, potatoes (maincrop), purple sprouting broccoli, radicchio, shallots, salsify, swede, wild garlic

April
Vegetables: Broccoli, cabbage, carrots, cauliflower, chard, chicory, cucumber, garlic, jersey royal new potatoes, kale, leeks, lettuces & salad leaves, St George mushrooms, mushrooms (cultivated), nettles, onions, potatoes (maincrop), purple sprouting broccoli, radicchio, samphire, salsify, spinach, watercress, wild garlic

May
Vegetables: Asparagus, broad beans, broccoli, cabbage, carrots, cauliflower, chard, cucumber, garlic (fresh), Jersey royal new potatoes, lettuces & salad leaves, Morel mushrooms, mushrooms (cultivated), nettles, new potatoes, onions, potatoes (maincrop), radishes, rocket, St George mushrooms, samphire, spinach, watercress, wild garlic

June

Vegetables: Artichokes (globe), asparagus, broad beans, broccoli, cabbage, cardoons, carrots, cauliflower, chard, courgettes, cucumber, garlic (fresh), Jersey royal new potatoes, kohlrabi, lettuces & salad leaves, Morel mushrooms, mushrooms (cultivated), nettles, new potatoes, onions, peas, potatoes (maincrop), radishes, rocket, samphire, spinach, spring onions, tomatoes (greenhouse) turnips, watercress, wild garlic

July

Vegetables: Artichokes (globe), asparagus, aubergine, beetroot, broad beans, cabbage, cardoons, carrots, cauliflower, courgettes, cucumber, fennel, French beans, garlic (fresh), kohlrabi, lettuces & salad leaves, mushrooms (cultivated), nettles, new potatoes, onions, peas, peppers, potatoes (maincrop), radishes, rocket, spring onions, summer black truffle, romanesco, runner beans, samphire, spinach, spring onions, sweetcorn, tomatoes (greenhouse), turnips, watercress

August

Vegetables: Artichokes (globe), aubergine, beetroot, broad beans, cabbage, cardoons, carrots, cauliflower, celery, cobnuts, courgettes, cucumber, fennel, French beans, garlic, kohlrabi, leeks, lettuces & salad leaves, marrow, mushrooms (cultivated), nettles, onions, peas, peppers, potatoes (maincrop), radishes, rocket, romanesco, runner beans, spinach, spring onions, tomatoes (outdoor), turnips, watercress, wild mushrooms

September

Vegetables: Artichokes (globe), aubergine, beetroot, broad beans, broccoli, butternut squash, cabbage, cardoons, carrots, celery, chicory, cobnuts, courgettes, cucumber, fennel, French beans, garlic, horseradish, kale, kohlrabi, leeks, lettuces & salad leaves, marrow, mushrooms (cultivated), nettles, onions, parsnips, peas, peppers, potatoes (maincrop), purple sprouting broccoli, radicchio, radishes, rocket, romanesco, runner beans, shallots, spinach, spring onions, swede, sweetcorn, tomatoes, turnips, walnuts, watercress, wild mushrooms

October   **Vegetables:** Beetroot, broccoli, Brussels sprouts, butternut squash, cabbage, cardoons, carrots, cauliflower, celeriac, chestnuts, chicory, cobnuts, cucumber, fennel, garlic, horseradish, Jerusalem artichokes, kale, kohlrabi, leeks, marrow, mushrooms (cultivated), onions, parsnips, peppers, potatoes (maincrop), pumpkin, purple sprouting broccoli, radicchio, radishes, rocket, romanesco, runner beans, salsify, shallots, spinach, spring onions, swede, sweetcorn, truffles (black), truffles (white), turnips, watercress, wild mushrooms

November   **Vegetables:** Beetroot, broccoli, brussels sprouts, cabbage, carrots, cauliflower, cardoons, celeriac, celery(blanched), chestnuts, chicory, garlic, horseradish, Jerusalem artichokes, kale, kohlrabi, leeks, mushrooms(cultivated), onions, parsnips, potatoes (maincrop), pumpkin, purple sprouting broccoli, radicchio, radishes, rocket, salsify, shallots, swede, sweetcorn, truffles (black), truffles (white), turnips, watercress, wild mushrooms

December   **Vegetables:** Beetroot, broccoli, Brussels sprouts, cabbage, carrots, cauliflower, celeriac, celery (blanched), chestnuts, chicory, garlic, horseradish, Jerusalem artichoke, kale, leeks, mushrooms (cultivated), onions, parsnips, potatoes (maincrop), purple sprouting broccoli, radicchio, radishes, salsify, shallots, swede, truffles (black), truffles (white), turnips, watercress, wild mushrooms

Grow Your Own Herbs

Herbs enable us to vary the flavour of familiar vegetables, meat and fish, their oils contributing wonderfully to the scent of the kitchen.

To use fresh herbs, the best option is to grow your own. This can easily be done on a kitchen windowsill as many herbs are available in seed form. Tarragon isn't, as the best, French form is only really available when taken from cuttings, but it can be bought widely as a plant from good nurseries.

If you are going to try to grow herbs from plants you buy in growing form, it is important to realise that herbs are usually grown in greenhouse conditions. This means that when you take the plant home, it will take some time to acclimatise to the conditions in your house.

The best way to acclimatise a herb plant to your home is to place it in a light and warm place, and not in full sunlight. Water the plant sparingly so that the compost remains lightly moist but do not give the plant so much water that it sits in water on its tray or saucer.

Stroke the plant regularly – releasing the smell will not only be pleasant to you but the activity will stimulate the plant to grow more strongly. This technique is commonly practised in the orient.

As the plant settles into the conditions of your home, you can move it to a sunnier place – the higher light conditions will stimulate the production of new growth and flavourful oils, which will mean that your herbs develop stronger flavours.

If you have a warm corner out of doors, most herbs can be grown out of doors in the summer.

Mrs Beeton recommends drying herbs in a hot oven, but our hot ovens are very different to the types she was familiar with. If you would like to dry herbs, the best thing to do is to pick herb tips just before they flower and dry them on a stainless steel or plastic rack in a warm, dry place. If you place oily herb cuttings in too hot a place, the oils will burn and become acrid.

SOUPS

A Note on Soups

Soups can be delicate and light – think of the vegetable soups of spring and summer – or substantial and rich, like the more complex, often meatier, soups of winter. Whatever the type of soup you are making, your aim is to capture the character of the main ingredient, be it a vegetable, meat or fish.

A base for a soup is usually made by stewing some vegetables in oil or butter before adding stock or milk to cook the ingredients. This should give the soup base a deep, intense flavour, which can be reinforced and freshened up with vegetables added toward the end of cooking. Peas or asparagus, however, should only be added at the last minute and cooked for a very short time to preserve their colour and flavour.

It is a common misconception that all soups need to be cooked for a long time. This is only the case when tougher cuts of meat are being used. Generally, a soup is cooked as soon as the vegetables are tender and suitable for puréeing.

When making a puréed soup, a jug blender or liquidiser is essential for achieving the smoothest result. Add the soup in small batches to the liquidiser or jug blender then run the machine for 2–3 minutes between additions. Pass the soup through a fine sieve or chinois (see glossary of cooking terms on page 93) into a clean pan before reheating or chilling over ice. The soup can then be finished with a little seasoning to taste and perhaps a small addition of cream or unsalted butter can be whisked in to enrich it. Remember, though, when making soups, to use seasoning lightly. A soup does not require the same level of salt as a sauce, so when tasting, be careful not to over-season.

CHANTILLY SOUP

✳ Serves 4 ✳ Preparation time 10 minutes ✳ Cooking time 20 minutes

Mrs Beeton features another green pea soup recipe in her book, which is much as you might expect a Victorian soup recipe to be. The peas are boiled for upwards of 2 hours, ham is added, presumably to give the soup some flavour after all that boiling, and the green colour comes from 2 handfuls of spinach thrown in just before serving. Her Chantilly soup, by contrast, is refreshingly clean. Other than refining Mrs Beeton's onions to a combination of shallots and leeks and varying the herbs, very little has been changed in this recipe. It is important to use young, tender peas, but we are fortunate today in that we have the option of using frozen, which are a good alternative.

30g unsalted butter

50g leek, finely chopped

1 small shallot, peeled and finely sliced

½ bay leaf

700ml light chicken stock (see page 83)

500g fresh or frozen young peas

few mint leaves

salt and freshly ground black pepper

Melt the butter in a saucepan over a low heat. Add the leek, shallot and bay leaf and cook gently for 10 minutes, ensuring that the vegetables do not colour. If they begin to brown, add a little water and, if necessary, turn the heat down.

Add the stock and turn the heat up to bring it to simmering. Then turn the heat to high, add the peas and bring to a boil.

Remove from the heat, leave to stand for 5 minutes then season to taste with salt and black pepper. Transfer the soup to the jug of a liquidiser and add the mint. Run the machine for 2–3 minutes to purée the soup to a very smooth consistency. Pass the soup through a fine sieve into a pan, heat gently, check the seasoning and serve immediately – or chill as quickly as possible to preserve the colour if using later.

ASPARAGUS SOUP

✳ Serves 4 ✳ Preparation time 15 minutes ✳ Cooking time 45 minutes

Mrs Beeton's original book contains two asparagus soups. The first is a complex affair containing beef, bacon and ale while the second is more economical, with a large amount of split peas to add bulk. This recipe takes elements from both and has been adapted to make a cleaner, more delicate soup that brings out the flavour of the asparagus. It is, however, only worth making when asparagus is in season in May and June.

50g unsalted butter

1 onion, peeled and roughly chopped

1 bay leaf

1 thyme sprig

50g potatoes, peeled and chopped into 5mm dice

600ml vegetable or light chicken stock (see page 83)

500g asparagus, washed and white ends trimmed by 2cm

salt and freshly ground black pepper

Place the butter in a saucepan over a medium heat. Add the onion and a pinch of salt and cook, stirring, until soft and transparent and just beginning to turn golden at the edges.

Add the bay leaf, thyme, diced potatoes and stock. Raise the heat to high and bring to a boil, then reduce the heat and allow the soup to simmer until the potato is tender.

Meanwhile, trim the tips of the asparagus to 10cm and chop the remaining stems into 1cm pieces. Reserve the tips but add the chopped stems to the soup and cook for 10 minutes, or until they are tender.

Now add the tips, and cook for 2–3 minutes, or until tender. Transfer the soup to the jug of a liquidiser and purée for 2–3 minutes. Pass the soup through a fine sieve into a clean saucepan and check the seasoning before warming through and serving.

PORTABLE SOUP

✳ Makes 750ml concentrated soup ✳ Preparation time 30 minutes ✳ Cooking time 8 hours (over 2 days)

A classic Mrs Beeton recipe, which required very little alteration. She adds the note that: 'Soup can be made in 5 minutes with this, by dissolving a small piece, about the size of a walnut, in a pint of warm water, and simmering for 2 minutes. Vermicelli, macaroni, or other Italian pastes, may be added.' This soup has an extended cooking time, first to extract the gelatine from the meat and bones, and then to reduce and concentrate it. Ask your butcher to chop the shin of beef into 2cm chunks and to cut the pigs' trotters in half for you.

6 tbsp sunflower oil

3kg shin of beef, cut into small chunks

2 pigs' trotters or veal knuckles, cut in half

small bunch thyme

2 bay leaves

3 onions, chopped into chunks

4 sticks celery, trimmed and chopped into chunks

2 carrots, chopped into chunks

2 blades mace

3 cloves

special equipment

a large stockpot and a temperature probe

Add 4 tbsp of the oil to a frying pan over a medium heat and fry the shin in batches until well browned. Transfer to a large stockpot and add the trotters, thyme and bay leaves. Place the remaining 2 tbsp of the oil into a frying pan over a medium heat and add the vegetables. Fry them until they are lightly browned and add them to the meat.

Add the mace and cloves to the stockpot along with enough cold water to cover the meat by 3cm. Turn the heat to low and cook, but do not let the soup boil or simmer. After 1 hour, a temperature probe dipped into the liquid should read 80–90°C. If not, adjust the heat under the stockpot.

Cook for 4–5 hours, or until the meat is very soft. Strain the soup through a fine sieve into a large bowl, cover and chill. When cold, skim any fat from the surface, return the soup to the cleaned stockpot and bring to a boil over a high heat until reduced in volume to approximately 750ml. Remove from the heat and leave to cool.

When the soup has set into a firm jelly, store in small containers each containing 100–125ml stock in the freezer. To make up the soup, simply empty a container into a small pan and add 300ml boiling water and a splash of sherry to make a tasty broth for two people.

LEEK & POTATO SOUP

✳ Serves 4 ✳ Preparation time 10 minutes ✳ Cooking time 15 minutes

Surprisingly, given her usual approach to household economy, Mrs Beeton only uses the white part of the leek for this soup. Perhaps she saved the green part for something else. Because the leeks we buy today are almost always young and tender, this recipe uses the whole thing. The cooking time here has been reduced from the hour required in the original recipe to just a few minutes. However, to obtain the silkiest texture you will need to slice the leeks very finely and purée the soup very well.

40g unsalted butter

400g trimmed leeks, green and white parts separated, both finely shredded

2 bay leaves

1 thyme sprig

300g potatoes, peeled and cut into 3–4cm cubes

500ml vegetable stock (see page 83)

200ml whole milk

2 tbsp chopped parsley

50ml single cream

grating of nutmeg, to taste

salt and freshly ground black pepper

Place a saucepan over low heat and add the butter. When it has melted add the finely shredded white part of the leek, the bay leaves and the thyme.

Cook, stirring, over a low heat for 5–10 minutes, until the leeks begin to sweat and release their juices. They should sizzle gently but not brown. Add the cubed potatoes, stock and milk and bring to a rapid simmer.

Cook until the potato is tender, then add the finely chopped leek greens and parsley and continue to simmer for 4–5 minutes, until the leek greens are just tender.

Transfer the soup to the jug of a liquidiser and purée for 2–3 minutes, then pass through a fine sieve into a clean pan over a medium heat. Pour in the cream and reheat gently, stirring constantly.

Season with salt and black pepper, and grate over some fresh nutmeg to taste before serving.

JERUSALEM ARTICHOKE & BACON SOUP

✳ Serves 4 ✳ Preparation time 15 minutes ✳ Cooking time 35 minutes

Winter soups rarely come better than this nutty, savoury soup. Mrs Beeton used milk in her artichoke soup, which would give a richer result than my version here. The bacon adds a savoury note, which is balanced by the sweet richness of the artichokes.

25g unsalted butter

90g streaky bacon, finely sliced

100g shallots, peeled and finely chopped

500g Jerusalem artichokes, peeled and cut into 2cm chunks (kept in water with a little lemon juice until required)

1 bay leaf

600ml vegetable stock (see page 83)

salt and freshly ground black pepper

Place the butter in a saucepan over medium heat. Add the bacon and cook until the fat has rendered and the bacon begins to crisp.

Using a slotted spoon, remove half of the bacon to a dish and reserve for finishing the soup. Add the shallots to the remaining bacon and stew for 5 minutes so that they soften but do not brown. If necessary, turn the heat down a little.

Add the artichokes along with the bay leaf and cook over a medium heat for 8–10 minutes, or until they begin to break down at the edges. If the vegetables begin to brown, or the bottom of the pan begins to darken and burn, turn the heat down and add a splash of cold water before continuing.

When the artichokes begin to soften, add the stock, turn the heat up to high and bring the mixture quickly to a boil. When the artichokes are tender, transfer the soup to the jug of a liquidiser and run the machine for 2–3 minutes, or until the mixture is very finely puréed.

Pass the soup through a very fine sieve back into the pan. Set the heat to medium, add the reserved bacon pieces and reheat the soup.

Season with salt and black pepper to taste and serve.

CHESTNUT & CELERIAC SOUP

✳ Serves 4 ✳ Preparation time 15 minutes ✳ Cooking time 40 minutes

Mrs Beeton's original chestnut soup recipe is updated here by the addition of celeriac and leek, which help to lighten it for the modern palate, yet give the soup a fully aromatic and velvety texture.

50g unsalted butter

1 onion, peeled and
finely chopped

100g finely sliced leek

400g celeriac, peeled and chopped
into 2cm chunks

150g cooked chestnuts, peeled

1 bay leaf

1 thyme sprig

600ml vegetable stock
(see page 83)

100ml milk

50ml single cream

salt and freshly ground
black pepper

Place the butter in a saucepan over a medium heat. Add the onion, leek and celeriac and cook gently for 10–15 minutes, until the vegetables begin to soften but do not brown. If they do, add a splash of water and turn the heat to low before continuing.

Add the chestnuts and cook very slowly for another 5 minutes, stirring frequently to prevent the chestnuts sticking to the bottom of pan.

Add the herbs, stock, milk and cream and turn the heat to medium, then simmer the soup until the vegetables are tender. This will take about another 10 minutes depending on how fresh the celeriac is.

Transfer the soup to the jug of a liquidiser and purée for 2–3 minutes, then pass through a fine sieve into a clean pan and warm over a medium heat. Season with salt and black pepper to taste and serve.

WILD DUCK & MUSHROOM BROTH

✳ Serves 4 ✳ Preparation time 15 minutes ✳ Cooking time 1 hour 15 minutes

This recipe is inspired by Mrs Beeton's regency soup, which is designed to use up 'any bones and remains of any cold game, such as of pheasants, partridges, etc'. Mushrooms, used here, particularly suit the flavour of wild duck. One leftover roast domestic duck leg would be roughly equivalent to the 4 wild duck legs listed in the ingredients. If you use raw duck legs, remove the skin and increase the initial cooking time for the legs to 1 hour.

4 wild duck legs leftover from roast ducks or raw

1 bay leaf

1 litre dark chicken stock or jellied game stock (see page 85 or 84)

2 tbsp light olive oil

2 large onions, peeled and finely chopped

100g (peeled weight) celeriac, finely chopped

80g carrot, peeled and chopped

10g butter

250g portobello mushrooms, sliced thickly

½ tsp thyme leaves

pinch ground allspice

salt and freshly ground black pepper

Place the duck legs, bay leaf and stock into a saucepan, bring to a simmer and then reduce the heat and put the lid on the pan. Cook for 45 minutes then remove from the heat.

Lift out the legs, leaving the liquid behind in the pan. When the legs are cool enough to handle, remove and discard the skin. Shred the meat and return it to the pan with the liquid.

Meanwhile, prepare the soup base. Place the oil in a saucepan over a medium heat. Add the onion and cook for 2–3 minutes, until it begins to sizzle a little. Add the celeriac, carrot and a pinch of salt. Reduce the heat and cook, stirring occasionally, for 10 minutes.

Set a frying pan over a medium heat and add the butter, the mushrooms and a pinch of salt. Cook, stirring, until the mushrooms begin to brown. Add them to the vegetables in the pan and then add the stock and duck meat, thyme and allspice.

Bring the broth to a simmer over a medium heat, season to taste and serve.

SHELLFISH BISQUE

✳ Makes 2 litres ✳ Preparation time 1 hour 30 minutes ✳ Cooking time 3–4 hours

This richly aromatic stock forms the foundation of delicious shellfish soups, such as bisque. The best shells to use are those left from picking crab and lobster. A fishmonger who sells dressed crabs will usually be happy to save you some shells in the freezer. Roasting the shells intensifies their flavour.

for the shellfish stock

2kg crab, lobster or prawn shells

2 tbsp sunflower oil

1 stick celery, roughly chopped

1 large onion, peeled and roughly chopped

1 medium carrot, peeled and roughly chopped

1 large tomato, roughly chopped

50ml brandy

300ml dry white Vermouth

500ml dry white wine

1 garlic clove, peeled and halved

2 bay leaves

1 large thyme sprig

for the bisque

50g onion, peeled and chopped

50g leek, chopped

50g carrot, peeled and chopped

50g celery, chopped

250ml double cream

500g fresh crab or lobster meat (optional)

salt, to taste

special equipment

a roasting tin and a stockpot

Preheat the oven to 200°C/gas mark 6. Place the shells in the tin, drizzle over the oil and toss to coat, then set in the oven to roast. Stir occasionally until beginning to brown.

After 1 hour add the celery, onion, carrot and tomato, and mix well. Roast for a further 30 minutes, stirring occasionally. Remove the tin from the oven and set on the cooker top.

Add the brandy to the tin and carefully set the mixture alight at the side of the tin using a match, tipping the liquid around the tin to catch all of the alcohol. Allow the flames to die down then add the wine and Vermouth. Stir the mixture together and scrape into the stockpot.

Pour in enough cold water to cover the shells to a depth of 10cm, then add the garlic and herbs to the pan and set over a high heat. Bring to a simmer, turn the heat down to low and cook for 3 hours. Strain the mixture into a bowl then pour it back into the cleaned stockpot and simmer until it is reduced to about 2 litres.

For the bisque, add the chopped vegetables to the stockpot and simmer for 5 minutes, then strain to remove the vegetables. Measure the stock, and for every 400ml, add 50ml of double cream.

Return the bisque to a clean pan and set on a medium heat. Warm the soup to a very gentle simmer, then taste for seasoning, adding a little salt if necessary. Stir through the fresh crab or lobster meat (if using), heat for another 2 minutes without boiling and serve immediately.

SALADS &
STARTERS

WATERCRESS SALAD

✳ Serves 4 ✳ Preparation time 10 minutes

Watercress and many other wild plants were so commonly collected and used historically that we rarely see recipes for them – they are simply taken for granted. Hampshire watercress came to prominence when the railways brought crops into the London markets at around the time Mrs Beeton's book was published, and it is still the best. This flavourful strong leaf is an ideal accompaniment to any game or meat dish.

4 large handfuls fresh watercress

3 tbsp extra virgin olive oil

juice of ¼ lemon

pinch sea salt

Place the watercress in a large bowl of iced water, and then pick the pieces out, discarding any tough stems as you go. Transfer the leaves to a salad spinner. Just before you are ready to serve, give the leaves a spin to dry them then place them in a salad bowl. Drizzle over the olive oil, a good squeeze of lemon and a little salt. Then toss gently to coat and serve.

GOAT CHEESE, RADISH & BROAD BEAN SALAD

✳ Serves 4 ✳ Preparation time 25 minutes ✳ Cooking time 2 minutes

Fresh cheeses, such as a soft, unrinded goat cheese, are just one step up from the curds and whey Mrs Beeton made. Goat cheese is the simplest type of cheese, and it is made all over the world. This superb, light salad shows how versatile fresh goat cheese can be.

for the dressing

1½ tbsp cider vinegar or good white wine vinegar

1 small shallot, peeled and finely chopped

pinch salt

6 tbsp extra virgin olive oil

1 tbsp finely chopped mint leaves

for the salad

100g baby broad beans, podded weight

75g radishes, trimmed and quartered

2 small handfuls picked watercress leaves

for the goat cheese mousse

200g fresh, unripened goat cheese

zest of ½ lemon

1 tbsp olive oil

1 tbsp milk

Start the dressing off by placing the vinegar in a small bowl and adding the shallot and a pinch of salt. Leave, covered, for 10 minutes while you prepare the salad ingredients.

Bring a small pan of salted water to boiling over a high heat. Add the broad beans and cook for 2 minutes, then drain and plunge into a bowl of iced water. Once cool, peel off the pale outer skins and place the beans into a large bowl. Add the radishes and watercress, toss to combine, cover and set aside.

Now prepare the mousse. Place the goat cheese, lemon zest, olive oil and milk in a bowl and beat well with a fork until light and fluffy enough to just hold its shape.

Finish the dressing by whisking the olive oil into the shallot and vinegar mixture. Stir in the mint, then pour over the salad ingredients and toss well.

Divide the goat cheese mousse between 4 plates and pile a portion of salad alongside the cheese, drizzling over any excess dressing. Serve with crusty bread.

GOAT CHEESE WITH LENTILS

✳ Serves 4 ✳ Preparation time 30 minutes ✳ Cooking time 45 minutes

Mrs Beeton noted how useful lentils are to those avoiding meat in their diet, though she also commented on their decline in British cooking. Lentils have since found favour again and here, combined with radicchio, they provide a lovely bed for a winter goat cheese salad.

1 quantity of braised Puy lentils (see page 59)

2 tsp sherry vinegar

2 tsp Dijon mustard

½ garlic clove, crushed

3 tbsp olive oil

small bunch flat-leaf parsley, leaves only, finely chopped

80g radicchio leaves, chopped into 2cm strips

160g ripened goat cheese, such as Tymsboro or Kidderton Ash, broken into 1cm pieces

lemon juice, to taste

salt and freshly ground black pepper

Make the braised Puy lentils, complete with the vegetables. Drain and set aside.

In a large bowl, whisk together the vinegar, mustard and garlic with a pinch of salt to taste. Add the oil in a thin trickle, whisking all the while until the mixture is emulsified.

Season the lentils with ¼ tsp salt and stir them into the oil mixture then add the parsley and radicchio. Fold all the ingredients together gently until evenly combined. Gently fold in the goat cheese pieces. Add a squeeze of lemon, season to taste and divide among the plates to serve.

EGGS BAKED WITH CREAM & TARRAGON

❋ Serves 4 ❋ Preparation time 10 minutes ❋ Cooking time 15–20 minutes

This is another variation on Mrs Beeton's poached eggs with cream. Here, rather than being poached, the eggs are baked with the cream and a little tarragon for added flavour.

butter, for greasing

1 French tarragon sprig

4 medium eggs

4 tbsp double cream

salt and freshly ground black pepper

special equipment

4 x 120ml ramekins and a roasting tin

Preheat the oven to 160°C/gas mark 3. Fill the kettle and bring it to boiling.

Butter the ramekins. Strip the leaves from the tarragon sprig and distribute them between the ramekins. Crack 1 egg into each ramekin and add a pinch of salt and a grinding of black pepper. Then pour 1 tbsp double cream into each ramekin.

Stand the ramekins in the roasting tin and carefully pour the boiling water into the tin around the ramekins to a depth of 2–3cm. Cover loosely with foil and bake for 15 minutes for a soft egg or 20 minutes for a firm egg. Serve immediately.

CHEESY PUFFS

✳ Serves 8–10 as a snack ✳ Preparation time 20 minutes ✳ Cooking time 20 minutes

Something of a leap from Mrs Beeton's traditional cheese straws in their texture and presentation, and yet retaining that moreish, tangy, cheesy flavour, these are wonderful party nibbles.

200g plain flour

salt

450ml milk

150g unsalted butter

6 large eggs, lightly beaten

200g strong Cheddar, such as Isle of Mull, coarsely grated

50g Parmesan cheese, finely grated

vegetable oil, for frying

special equipment

a deep-fryer

Sift the flour and a generous pinch of salt together into a large bowl. Place the milk and butter into a saucepan over a medium heat. Bring to boiling and then pour in all of the flour, stirring well until the mixture comes away from the sides of the pan and forms a ball in the centre. Transfer this mixture back into the large bowl and leave to cool for 5 minutes.

Add the eggs to the flour paste a little bit at a time, beating well with each addition until all the eggs have been added and the mixture is shiny. Add the Cheddar and half the Parmesan and stir well to amalgamate.

Preheat the oven to low and preheat the deep-fryer to 170°C. Line a baking sheet with a double layer of kitchen paper and place it in the oven. Drop teaspoonfuls of the mixture into the hot oil, cooking no more than 8 at a time. They are cooked when the balls are a deep dark brown all over. Lift them from the oil using a slotted spoon and place them on the lined baking sheet in the oven to drain well. Repeat until all of the mixture is used up, then place the puffs onto a serving dish and sprinkle with the remaining Parmesan cheese and serve hot.

CHEESE SOUFFLÉ

✳ Serves 4 ✳ Preparation time 40 minutes ✳ Cooking time 8–10 minutes

This is great served with the cheese, or as a course in itself – just make sure your guests are in place at the table and ready to eat as soon as the soufflé emerges from the oven.

25g unsalted butter, plus extra for greasing

85g strong cheese such as Isle of Mull Cheddar or Parmesan, finely grated, plus extra for dusting

120ml milk

½ small onion, peeled and sliced

½ tsp black peppercorns

½ bay leaf

very small carrot, peeled and chopped

25g plain flour

1 tsp Dijon mustard

2 large eggs, separated, plus 1 egg white

special equipment

4 x 120ml ramekins and a roasting tin

Butter the ramekins, ensuring the butter covers the rim as well, dust with a little finely grated cheese and set aside.

Place the milk, onion, peppercorns, bay leaf and carrot in a medium saucepan and bring to boiling over a medium heat. As soon as the mixture boils remove from the heat and leave for the flavour to infuse for 30 minutes.

Meanwhile, melt the butter in a small pan over a medium heat. When it foams add the flour and cook, stirring gently, for 3–4 minutes. Do not let the flour burn – if it begins to turn brown at the edges, dip the base of the pan in cold water to halt the cooking process.

Strain the infused milk into a pan, discarding the vegetables and herbs, and bring to a simmer over a medium heat. Place the pan with the flour mixture back on a low heat and whisk in the hot milk mixture a little at a time, allowing it to simmer after each addition. Once all the milk has been added, simmer the sauce for 3–5 minutes, then add the cheese and mustard and continue to whisk over a low heat until the cheese is melted and the mixture is glossy. Remove from the heat and add the egg yolks, stirring quickly.

Preheat the oven to 200°C/gas mark 6 and boil the kettle. Place the egg whites into a clean, stainless steel bowl and whisk until they form soft peaks. Fold one-third of the egg whites into the cheese mixture, then gently fold all of the cheese mixture back into the remaining egg whites.

Place the ramekins in the roasting tin and divide the mixture between them. Pour the boiling water into the tin to a depth of 2cm. Bake the soufflés for 8–10 minutes until they are well risen and golden. Serve immediately.

MUSHROOM RAGOUT

✳ Serves 4 as a starter ✳ Preparation time 5 minutes ✳ Cooking time 25 minutes

This is a light dish that serves four as a snack or starter or as an accompaniment to grilled meat or poultry. If you have access to seasonal wild mushrooms from a reliable source then replace the chestnut mushrooms with a selection of whatever is available. Mrs Beeton used lemon in her mushrooms, so she also added flour to prevent the sauce curdling. A similar result is achieved here using cream and a little sherry, which allows the fine taste of the mushrooms to come through.

50g unsalted butter

2 shallots, peeled and finely chopped

250g chestnut mushrooms, wiped and cut into quarters

1 garlic clove, finely chopped

1 thyme sprig

20ml sherry

50ml white wine

300ml dark chicken stock (see page 85)

100ml double cream

bunch flat-leaf parsley, stems discarded, leaves finely chopped

salt and freshly ground black pepper

Place the butter in a large frying pan over a low heat, add the shallots and fry gently, stirring, for 3–4 minutes until they soften. Add the mushrooms, garlic, thyme, sherry and white wine and simmer for 5 minutes until the liquid has reduced to nothing. Pour in the stock and cook for 10 minutes, or until it has reduced by two-thirds. Add the double cream and simmer gently until reduced by half and thickened to a creamy consistency. Season with salt and black pepper to taste then stir the parsley through the mushrooms and serve.

BOILED &
BRAISED VEG

GLOBE ARTICHOKES

✳ Serves 4 ✳ Preparation time 15 minutes ✳ Cooking time approx 45 minutes

This is an uncomplicated way of enjoying one of the most delicious vegetables it is possible to grow in our climate. Mrs Beeton recommended serving artichokes in several ways, but try this one first. Use mature artichokes, which are easy to find.

4 large globe artichokes

1 tbsp salt

1 lemon, sliced

50ml light olive oil

1 quantity hollandaise sauce (see page 86), to serve

special equipment

4 ramekins or small bowls

Prepare the artichokes by trimming the stems just beneath the base of the globe. Using a pair of scissors, trim any spikes from the leaves. Wash well and check closely for dirt.

Choose a pan that will hold all of the artichokes at once. Fill it half full with water, add the salt, cover and bring to a boil over a high heat. When the water is boiling, add the lemon and olive oil and drop in the artichokes.

Cover the pan and bring to a simmer. Cook over a low heat for 35–45 minutes, depending on the size and age of the artichokes. Meanwhile, make the hollandaise sauce and keep it warm in a bowl suspended over a pan of hot water until ready to use.

The artichokes are done when you can pierce the base easily with a thin knife and a lower leaf pulls off easily. Drain the artichokes upside down on a wire rack placed over a bowl for 10 minutes.

To serve, place each artichoke upright on a plate and provide each person with a bowlful of hollandaise sauce.

To eat, pull the leaves from the artichokes individually, dip each one into the sauce and then scrape the fleshy part of the leaf onto your tongue using your front teeth. Discard the leaf. Pull all of the leaves off in this way. When you get to the centre, discard the choke (the fibrous part) and eat the solid base of the artichoke.

JERUSALEM ARTICHOKES
WITH BACON & CREAM

✳ Serves 4 as a starter or 6 as a side dish ✳ Preparation time 15 minutes ✳ Cooking time 25–30 minutes

Mrs Beeton serves this richly flavoured, sweet-tasting vegetable with a white sauce. The additional touch of bacon here marries perfectly with the sweet vegetables.

25g unsalted butter

150g dry cured bacon, cut into small strips

150g shallots, peeled and finely sliced

2 bay leaves

1 large sprig thyme, leaves only

700g peeled Jerusalem artichokes

250ml double cream

salt and freshly ground black pepper

Melt the butter in a saucepan over a medium heat, then add the bacon and fry gently until it renders its fat and begins to brown a little at the edges. Add the shallots, bay leaves and thyme and cook, stirring, for 3–4 minutes, until the vegetables begin to release their juices, then stir in the artichokes. Add 200ml water to the pan and bring to a simmer, then cover with a lid, turn the heat down low and cook for 10 minutes, stirring occasionally. Poke the artichokes with a skewer to test them for tenderness. When they are just beginning to soften, add the cream, turn the heat up and cook uncovered until the artichokes are soft and the cream is reduced to a coating sauce. Season with a little salt and black pepper and serve.

CARROT & SWEDE MASH

✳ Serves 4 ✳ Preparation time 10 minutes ✳ Cooking time 20–25 minutes

Carrots and turnips (the family to which the swede belongs) were popular 150 years ago and remain so today. Mrs Beeton offered several options for each; this recipe goes further and combines the two, seasoning with nutmeg, which often featured in her carrot dishes.

350g swede, peeled and cut into 2cm dice

350g carrots, peeled and cut into 2cm dice

30g unsalted butter

salt and freshly ground black pepper

large pinch grated nutmeg

Put 1 litre water in a saucepan over a high heat. Add 1 tsp salt and bring to a boil. Add the swede and simmer for 10 minutes, then add the carrot and continue to simmer for a further 10 minutes, or until both vegetables are tender.

Drain off as much water as you can and then add the butter, along with plenty of freshly ground black pepper and a large pinch of freshly grated nutmeg. Mash well with a potato masher, transfer to a serving dish and serve.

BRAISED CELERY

✳ Serves 4 ✳ Preparation time 10 minutes ✳ Cooking time 1 hour

This makes a first-rate accompaniment for winter roast chicken or game. Mrs Beeton used traditional white celery and cooked it with milk or cream, but our modern green varieties have a stronger flavour, which calls for a more flavoursome cooking liquor.

6 sticks celery weighing approx 400g in total

350ml light chicken stock (see page 83)

1 bay leaf

¼ tsp salt

special equipment

a shallow ovenproof dish

Preheat the oven to 160°C/gas mark 3. Cut each celery stick into 3 even pieces and arrange them in a single layer in a shallow ovenproof dish. Bring the stock to a gentle simmer in a small saucepan over a medium heat. Add the bay leaf and salt, then pour the mixture over the celery. Cover the dish with greaseproof paper, then tightly wrap with foil and place in the oven for 1 hour. It is cooked when the celery can be easily pierced with the tip of a knife. Serve immediately.

BRAISED BEETROOT

✳ Serves 4 ✳ Preparation time 10 minutes ✳ Cooking time 1 hour 15 minutes

Deeply aromatic, braised beetroot accompanies pork, game or fish dishes superbly. Mrs Beeton suggested stewing some onions with the beetroot. If you like, add 100g peeled shallots or small onions to the pan with the beetroot in the second stage of their cooking.

500g young beetroot, topped and tailed

large pinch Maldon sea salt or other flaky salt

1 garlic clove, peeled and finely chopped

40g unsalted butter

100ml dark chicken stock (see page 85)

salt and freshly ground black pepper

Preheat the oven to 180°C/gas mark 4. Place the beetroot on a large sheet of foil and sprinkle over the salt and garlic. Shape the foil into a parcel around the ingredients and seal it well. Place on a baking tray and bake in the oven for 1 hour. Remove from the oven, open the parcel and allow the beetroot to cool. When they are cool enough to handle, peel and cut each one into 8 evenly-sized pieces.

To finish the dish, melt the butter in a saucepan over a medium heat. Add the beetroot and stir to coat with the butter. Raise the heat and add the stock, simmering to reduce it to a syrupy glaze. Season with salt and black pepper and serve.

BRAISED RED CABBAGE

✳ Serves 6–8 ✳ Preparation time 30 minutes ✳ Cooking time 2 hours

Mrs Beeton's recipe for red cabbage calls for a mixture of vinegar and sugar to give piquancy to this wonderful vegetable. I have added spice and a little fresh apple to lighten it. This can be used as a dish in its own right, served with good bread and butter, but it also makes a beautiful accompaniment to pork and poultry dishes.

25g salted butter

1 onion, peeled and finely chopped

250g peeled and cored cooking apples, diced small

1 x 500g red cabbage, quartered, cored and finely shredded

1 cinnamon stick

2 cloves

seeds from 4 cardamom pods

2 tsp English honey

1 tsp red wine vinegar

100ml red wine

salt and freshly ground black pepper

Preheat the oven to 160°C/gas mark 3.

Place the butter in a large pan over a low heat. Add the chopped onion together with a large pinch of salt and cook, stirring, for 5 minutes, until the onion is soft and beginning to colour a little at the edges. Turn the heat to medium, add all the remaining ingredients and combine well.

Place the mixture in an ovenproof dish and press down to an even thickness. Cover the dish with a sheet of greaseproof paper and then seal with a layer of foil. Transfer the dish to the oven and cook for about 2 hours, or until the cabbage is tender, stirring occasionally. Season to taste with salt and black pepper before serving.

HARICOT BEANS

✳ Serves 4 ✳ Preparation time 5 minutes plus 12 hours soaking time ✳ Cooking time 1 hour 15 minutes

Mrs Beeton's method for white haricot beans has been adapted here to work with any dried bean. Do make sure your beans are as fresh as possible. This means they will plump up and become tender without having to be cooked for an enormous length of time.

150g dried haricot beans

1 carrot, peeled and cut into tiny dice

1 onion, peeled and finely chopped

1 stick celery, trimmed and finely chopped

3 garlic cloves, peeled and left whole

1 bay leaf

1 large thyme sprig

100ml extra virgin olive oil, plus 3 tbsp extra to finish

small bunch flat-leaf parsley, leaves and fine stalks only

salt and freshly ground black pepper

Place the beans in a large bowl, cover them with cold water and leave to soak overnight. The next day, drain and pick over the beans, discarding any that have not swollen, any that are discoloured and any foreign objects. Place the beans in a large pan over a medium heat, cover with cold water and bring to a simmer. Skim off any foam from the surface then add half the carrot, half the onion, half the celery, 2 garlic cloves, the bay leaf and the thyme. Simmer gently for up to 1 hour, or until almost tender. The time this takes will depend on the age of the beans. Add more boiling water as necessary to ensure that they are always covered. Once cooked, drain and discard the liquid.

Place 100ml olive oil in a large saucepan over a low heat and add the remaining vegetables. Fry gently, stirring occasionally, for 7–8 minutes, or until they are soft but not coloured. Add the beans and enough water to cover. Simmer gently until the beans are very tender, topping the pan up with boiling water as necessary so that they always remain covered. Remove the pan from the heat, add a pinch of salt and leave the beans to absorb their seasoning for 5 minutes. Taste and adjust the seasoning if necessary, then fish out and discard the bay leaf and thyme sprig.

If you are not using the beans immediately, they will keep for 3–4 days in their liquid, in an airtight container in the fridge.

To serve, drain the beans from the liquid and place in a serving dish. Drizzle over 3 tbsp olive oil. Finely chop the parsley and the remaining garlic clove together, stir this mixture through the beans and serve.

BRAISED PUY LENTILS

✳ Serves 4 ✳ Preparation time 20 minutes ✳ Cooking time 45 minutes

Mrs Beeton notes how useful lentils and beans are for meat-free times, Lent especially. Many people now choose not to eat meat, but even meat-eaters will enjoy this lovely recipe. These lentils are used as the base for the goat cheese with lentils recipe on page 39, but they are also ideal for serving with roast goose or any game dish.

200g Puy lentils

3 tbsp olive oil

½ onion, peeled and finely chopped

1 small carrot, peeled and finely chopped

½ stick celery, trimmed and finely chopped

1 bay leaf

1 thyme sprig

2 garlic cloves, finely chopped

small bunch flat-leaf parsley, stems discarded, leaves finely chopped

3 tbsp extra virgin olive oil

salt and freshly ground black pepper

Place the lentils in a medium-sized pan over a high heat and add 1.5 litres of water. Bring to a boil then turn down and simmer for 10 minutes, or until just tender. Drain and set aside.

Put the olive oil in a large frying pan over a low heat and add the onion, carrot, celery, bay leaf, thyme and half the chopped garlic. Cook for 10 minutes, or until the vegetables begin to soften. Then add the lentils and enough fresh water to cover everything.

Let the mixture simmer very gently for 20–25 minutes. Then remove the pan from the heat and drain the mixture into a sieve, discarding the liquid and the bay leaf. Place the lentil mixture into a serving dish and stir in the remaining chopped garlic and the parsley. Drizzle over the extra virgin olive oil, season to taste with salt and black pepper and serve.

YELLOW SPLIT PEAS WITH SMOKED BACON

✳ Serves 4 ✳ Preparation time 5 minutes ✳ Cooking time 1 hour 30 minutes

Mrs Beeton uses split peas in her pease pudding, which she comments 'should always be sent to table with boiled leg of pork'. Here, the pork (in the form of bacon) is combined with the peas to make a modern take on pease pudding, which also has the advantage of being far quicker to cook than the original. It is an inspired accompaniment for a roast.

350g yellow split peas

1 bay leaf

25g melted butter

100g smoked bacon, cut into small pieces

small bunch parsley, thick stems discarded, leaves finely chopped

salt and freshly ground black pepper

Put the peas and bay leaf in a saucepan over a medium to high heat, cover with water and bring to a boil, stirring. Reduce the heat and simmer for 1 hour, or until the peas are tender. Drain through a sieve, fish out and discard the bay leaf and set the peas aside.

Place the butter in another saucepan over a medium heat. Add the bacon and fry until it begins to render its fat and colours a little at the edges. Then reduce the heat, add the peas and toss everything together. Season to taste with a little salt, if needed, and some black pepper. Stir the parsley through, transfer to a dish and serve.

MASHED POTATOES

✳ Serves 4 ✳ Preparation time 10 minutes ✳ Cooking time 35 minutes

Mrs Beeton gave several recipes for different methods of making mashed potato, reflecting perhaps that we all seem to have our favourite method. Make them as soft and buttery as you like, using this recipe as a starting point.

650–700g peeled Maris piper or King Edward potatoes, cut into 3cm cubes

10g salt

130g butter

1 tbsp milk

salt and freshly ground black pepper

Place the potatoes in a large saucepan, add enough water to cover and the salt. Bring to a boil over a high heat, then reduce the heat and simmer very gently for about 20 minutes, checking them regularly with a sharp knife. As soon as they are tender, remove from the heat.

Drain through a large colander. To ensure any excess water is driven off, leave the potatoes to sit, uncovered, until quite dry and still warm, then return them to the pan.

Melt the butter in a small pan over a medium heat. When it is hot and foaming add the milk and stir, then pour the mixture over the potatoes. Turn the heat under the potatoes to medium and mash them with a potato masher to break them up,then beat them with a wooden spoon until light and fluffy. Alternatively, melt the butter in a larger pan and then press the potatoes through a ricer onto the hot butter and milk, beating after that with a wooden spoon. Adjust the seasoning to taste, and serve piping hot.

STOVED POTATOES

✳ Serves 4 ✳ Preparation time 5 minutes ✳ Cooking time 25–35 minutes, depending on size

Really fresh new potatoes are still a seasonal treat, and Jersey Mids, which appear in March, command a high price. This recipe concentrates their delicious flavour.

600g small new potatoes or Jersey Mids, as fresh as possible

50g unsalted butter

1 tsp snipped chives, to serve

salt and freshly ground black pepper

Place the potatoes in a saucepan. Add the butter, a large pinch of salt and enough water to cover and bring to a boil over a high heat, then turn down and leave to simmer gently for 15–20 minutes. Shake the pan occasionally to ensure the potatoes cook evenly.

When they are almost tender, raise the heat to reduce the liquid to a glaze. Transfer to a serving dish, sprinkle with the chives, season and serve.

GLAZED TURNIPS

✳ Serves 4 ✳ Preparation time 15 minutes ✳ Cooking time 20 minutes

This is a version of Mrs Beeton's so-called 'German method of cooking turnips' and is a super way with this underrated vegetable. Turnips, as opposed to swede, can be grown at any time of the year, but in the late spring, harvested when they are still at the 'baby' stage, they are at their most juicy and tender.

300g small purple- or white-topped turnips

2 tbsp light olive oil

300ml light chicken stock (see page 83)

25g unsalted butter

salt and freshly ground black pepper

Peel and top and tail the turnips and trim off any dark or bruised parts. Cut into small wedges about 1.5cm thick and set aside.

Place the oil in a large frying pan over a high heat. Add the turnip wedges and a pinch of salt and fry, stirring, until they are lightly browned. Add the stock, reduce the heat to low and cover. Simmer gently for about 10 minutes, or until the turnips are almost tender, then remove the lid and add the butter. Turn the heat up a little and cook until the liquid is reduced to a nice glaze. Season to taste with salt and black pepper and serve.

POTATO & CREAM GRATIN

✳ Serves 4 ✳ Preparation time 20 minutes ✳ Cooking time 1 hour

Mrs Beeton used gravy rather than cream in her 'German method of cooking potatoes', adding a bay leaf to improve the flavour. Here, cream makes the dish more luxurious, and avoids any conflict of flavours if you are serving the gratin with another dish.

20g unsalted butter,
for greasing

600g peeled and thinly sliced
King Edward potatoes

400ml single cream

2 large pinches ground mace

2 bay leaves

2 garlic cloves, sliced

salt and freshly ground
black pepper

special equipment

a shallow 1.5-litre
ovenproof dish

Preheat the oven to 200°C/gas mark 6 and butter the ovenproof dish. Wash the potato slices in several changes of water, drain and set aside.

Pour the cream into a large, shallow pan over a medium heat and add the mace, bay leaves, garlic, ½ tsp salt and freshly ground black pepper to taste. Bring to a gentle simmer, and then add the potatoes. Cook, stirring, until the cream begins to simmer and thicken. Taste for seasoning and add a little more salt, mace and freshly ground black pepper, if necessary. As the potatoes begin to cook they will absorb the salt from the cream so season it assertively.

Pour the contents of the pan into the prepared dish, pressing the potatoes into an even layer. Bake in the centre of the oven. After 45 minutes remove the dish from the oven and leave to rest in a warm place for 5 minutes before serving.

GRILLED &
ROASTED VEG

ROAST CHICORY WITH PEARS

✳ Serves 4 ✳ Preparation time 10 minutes ✳ Cooking time 1 hour 20 minutes

Mrs Beeton recommends that any seasoning used with endive (or chicory) should be delicate: this pale, white vegetable is almost more texture than flavour, though you can detect a lovely hint of bitterness when it is roasted. The original recipe calls for a mixture of stock, lemon juice and sugar, but the addition of soft, fruity pears, which appear in our shops at the same time of year as the first home-grown chicory, balance the light bitterness beautifully. This is an excellent accompaniment to game or pork dishes.

40g unsalted butter, plus extra for greasing

2 heads white chicory, cut in half lengthways

50ml dark chicken or jellied game stock (see page 85 or 84)

pinch of salt

10g caster sugar

1 tsp lemon juice

2 large semi-ripe pears, peeled and quartered

1 tsp chopped thyme leaves

special equipment

a gratin dish

Preheat the oven to 200°C/gas mark 6 and butter the gratin dish. Place the chicory halves into the dish in a single layer, cut-side down, and bake for 30 minutes, or until the chicory has begun to release its juice. Turn them a couple of times during cooking to help them brown a little on all sides.

Remove from the oven and add the chicken stock, salt, sugar and lemon juice. Cook for a further 30 minutes, until the stock reduces, still turning the chicory occasionally.

Remove from the oven and add the pears, tossing everything together to coat the pears with the buttery juices. Sprinkle over the chopped thyme and cook for 20 minutes or until the pears are tender. Serve immediately.

CONFIT OF PARSNIPS

✳ Serves 4 ✳ Preparation time 10 minutes ✳ Cooking time 1 hour

Mrs Beeton herself was not particularly adventurous with parsnips, although she did report that they had been used successfully to make both bread and wine. As a vegetable, they did not come into their own until the years of World War II, when their sweetness was suddenly craved by a nation starved of sugar. This recipe is based on a method suggested for carrots or turnips, but uses ingredients that heighten the natural sweetness of the parsnips.

800g parsnips

75g softened unsalted butter

250ml fresh orange juice

1 tbsp English honey

1 tsp chopped fresh thyme

salt and freshly ground black pepper

special equipment

a roasting tin

Preheat the oven to 200°C/gas mark 6. Cut the parsnips in half crossways, then halve the thinner root end lengthways, and quarter the thicker top end lengthways. This will give you 6 roughly equal-sized pieces per parsnip.

Place 1 litre of water into a saucepan over a high heat. Add ½ tsp fine salt and bring to a boil. Add the parsnips and boil for 15–20 minutes, or until tender and the point of a knife will easily slip through the pieces.

Remove from the heat and drain. When they are cool enough to handle take a sharp knife and remove and discard the core from the quartered pieces of parsnip.

Place the parsnip pieces in a single layer on the roasting tin, add the remaining ingredients and stir everything around to coat. Bake, turning regularly, for 45 minutes, or until all of the liquid has evaporated and the parsnips are plump and lightly browned. Remove from the oven as soon as the parsnips are ready, so that the honey doesn't burn, and serve.

CAULIFLOWER PARMESAN

✳ Serves 4 ✳ Preparation time 15 minutes ✳ Cooking time 50 minutes

Mrs Beeton used Parmesan cheese to flavour her cauliflower gratin, but you can substitute any strongly flavoured, dry cheese you like, such as Isle of Mull Cheddar. Avoid Cheddar coated in wax, though, which tends to be too soft.

1 quantity béchamel sauce (see page 89)

600g cauliflower, tough leaves discarded

½ tsp English mustard powder

100g finely grated Parmesan cheese

salt and freshly ground black pepper

special equipment

a large ovenproof dish

Make the béchamel sauce according to the recipe and keep it warm until you need it.

Trim the ends off the pale inner leaves of the cauliflower, and cut them into 3cm lengths. Cut the cauliflower florets into 2–3cm chunks. Place 1 litre of water in a saucepan over a high heat and add a large pinch of salt. When the water boils, add the cauliflower florets and trimmed leaves and simmer for about 5 minutes, or until tender to the tip of a sharp knife. Drain well, transfer to an ovenproof dish and arrange in a layer 5–6cm thick.

Preheat the grill to medium-high. Add the mustard and two-thirds of the Parmesan to the béchamel sauce and mix well until smooth, then season with salt and black pepper.

Pour the sauce over the cauliflower, ensuring all the cauliflower is covered. Sprinkle the top with the remaining cheese and place under the grill. Cook for 4–5 minutes, or until the top is well browned and bubbling, and serve.

GRILLED MUSHROOMS
WITH GARLIC BUTTER

✳ Serves 4 ✳ Preparation time 10 minutes ✳ Cooking time 8–10 minutes

Mrs Beeton noted that large mushroom flaps (or tops) are best for this recipe, while she reserved button mushrooms for stews. Of course, you can use whichever you prefer, but the larger, mature mushrooms do have a more intense, almost animal flavour. You can grill them simply with butter and perhaps a sprinkle of lemon juice, as in the original recipe, but the addition of garlic gives a rich, savoury flavour.

50g softened unsalted butter

small bunch of parsley, leaves only, finely chopped

1 garlic clove, finely chopped

pinch Maldon or other flaky salt

8 large, flat field mushrooms, each about 8–10cm in diameter

2 tbsp olive oil, for brushing

salt and freshly ground black pepper

Preheat the grill to high. Place the butter in a medium-sized bowl and whip until creamy, pale and fluffy. Add the parsley, garlic and salt and whip until combined.

Peel the mushrooms and remove their stalks. Place them on a baking tray in a single layer gill-side down. Brush the caps with the olive oil, season with a light sprinkling of salt and place under the grill at a distance of no less than 10cm from the element. Cook until the mushrooms start to collapse and turn golden brown. Flip them over, divide the parsley and garlic butter between the mushrooms, then place them back under the grill and cook for 2 minutes, or until the butter is foaming and beginning to colour. Serve immediately.

POTATOES A LA MAITRE D'HOTEL

✳ Serves 4 ✳ Preparation time 10 minutes ✳ Cooking time 25 minutes

Charlotte potatoes or small new potatoes, both of which have less starch than other varieties, are just right for making this special recipe. The 'maître d'hôtel' combination of butter, lemon and parsley is one of Mrs Beeton's most commonly used flavourings.

400g small Charlotte or new potatoes

3 tbsp light olive oil

50g butter

1 banana shallot, peeled and chopped

100ml light chicken stock (see page 83)

finely grated zest of ½ lemon

large handful flat-leaf parsley, stems discarded, leaves finely chopped

salt and freshly ground black pepper

Place the potatoes in a large pan over a high heat. Cover them with water and add a large pinch of salt. Bring to a boil and cook for 10 minutes, or until the potatoes are tender, then drain well. Place the oil in a large frying pan over a medium to heat and fry the potatoes for 5–7 minutes, or until they lightly browned on all sides. Stir them occasionally to prevent them burning.

Season the potatoes with salt and black pepper then reduce the heat and add the butter and shallot to the pan. Toss gently together for 2 minutes to cook the shallot then add the stock. Continue cooking until the liquid is reduced to a glaze.

Remove the pan from the heat and transfer the potatoes to a serving dish. Add the lemon zest and parsley and toss everything together gently to combine. Serve immediately.

ROAST POTATOES

✳ Serves 4 ✳ Preparation time 30 minutes ✳ Cooking time 1 hour 30 minutes

Mrs Beeton only mentioned roast potatoes in passing: she cooked them in front of the fire, and noted that they should be sent to the table with additional cold butter. Of course, it is now more convenient to roast potatoes inside the oven according to the instructions in this recipe.

800g peeled potatoes cut into 3–4cm cubes

100g goose fat or dripping

salt

special equipment

a large roasting tin

Preheat the oven to 220°C/gas mark 7.

Place the potatoes in a large saucepan over a medium to high heat and cover them with water. Add 1 tsp salt and bring to a light boil. After 15 minutes remove from the heat and drain well. Shake the colander a few times to ruffle the edges of the potatoes, which will give them a crisper skin after roasting.

When you are ready to roast the potatoes, put the goose fat or dripping in the roasting tin and place in the oven just until the fat melts, then arrange the potatoes in the melted fat and return the tin to the oven. Turn the potatoes every 20 minutes. After 60 minutes, reduce the heat to 180°C/gas mark 4 and cook for a further 30 minutes, or until the potatoes are crisp and brown. Meanwhile, line a baking tray with kitchen paper and keep it handy near the oven. When the potatoes have finished roasting,remove them from the oven and switch the oven off. Using a pair of tongs, lift the potatoes out of the fat and onto the prepared baking tray. Place them back in the oven for 5 minutes to finish draining and serve.

STOCKS &
SAUCES

A Note on Stocks

Stocks are the foundation of many dishes, so it is worth ensuring that they contain only the best ingredients.

Bones should be fresh and trimmed of any excess fat. Those that have a good proportion of cartilage, such as knuckles, feet and ribs, are excellent for stock as the gelatine they contain gives the stock body. Pigs' trotters and calves' feet should be cut in half so that the gelatine is more easily released – get your butcher to do this.

Vegetables should be good quality and fresh. Wash them well and peel them if necessary before chopping or trimming them. Unless the recipe specifies otherwise always use medium-sized vegetables.

Herbs should be tied together in small bundles (called faggots in Mrs Beeton's day) using kitchen string so they are easy to retrieve from the stock once it has finished cooking.

Cold water, rather than hot, should be added to stocks as it encourages fat to rise and solidify, making it easier to skim from the surface.

Wine, if you use it, should be of drinking quality and not dregs or anything past its best.

Salt should only be added at the end. As you reduce the stock it will intensify the natural salts within the ingredients, so you should never add salt until the stock is fully reduced and you have tasted it. You can always add more seasoning at a later stage, if desired, but you cannot repair over-salted stock.

Stockpots

It is most efficient, and worthwhile, to make stock in large quantities, and for this you will need a large, stainless steel stockpot. A pot of 25–30cm in diameter that will hold 17 litres can be accommodated by most domestic hobs.

LIGHT CHICKEN STOCK

✳ Makes 1.5 litres ✳ Preparation time 10 minutes ✳ Cooking time 3 hours

Light chicken stock is used in delicately flavoured dishes, which would be masked by a more intensely flavoured stock. It is also useful for lighter soups, or for braising young vegetables such as turnips or beetroot.

1.5kg chicken wings and thighs, raw

1 large carrot, roughly chopped

2 onions, roughly chopped

2 sticks celery, roughly chopped

2 bay leaves

small bunch thyme

special equipment

a large stockpot

Place all the ingredients into the stockpot over a medium heat. Cover with cold water to a depth of 5–10cm and bring to a gentle simmer. Continue to simmer for 2 hours, making sure the stock does not boil at any point and skimming as necessary. Strain the stock through a fine sieve or chinois into a large bowl. Leave it to cool, then cover and chill.

Carefully remove any fat from the top of the chilled stock and pour it back into the cleaned stockpot. Bring to a boil over a high heat to reduce the stock until you are left with 1.5 litres. Remove from the heat and cool, then pour into re-sealable 250ml containers and freeze for up to 2 months.

VEGETABLE STOCK

✳ Makes 4 litres ✳ Preparation time 20 minutes ✳ Cooking time 1 hour

This quick, light and fragrant stock is ideal for making vegetable soups and other vegetarian dishes. Vegetable trimmings can be added to the base ingredients, but make sure that they are washed well and that any onion skins you use are free from mould.

4 onions, roughly chopped

2 leeks, roughly chopped

3 carrots, roughly chopped

1 stick celery, roughly chopped

1 large thyme sprig

3 bay leaves

special equipment

a large stockpot

Place all the ingredients into a large stockpot over a high heat. Add 4 litres of water and bring to a gentle simmer, then turn the heat down low and continue to simmer. After 1 hour strain the stock through a sieve into a large bowl, discarding the vegetables and flavourings. Cover and chill.

Once cold, pour the stock into re-sealable 250ml containers and freeze for up to 2 months.

JELLIED GAME STOCK

✳ Makes 2 litres ✳ Preparation time 1 hour 45 minutes ✳ Cooking time 8 hours

The backbones of game birds can be bitter, so do not use them in stocks. When using giblets, always check them for green or yellow stains. These indicate contamination with bile, and any affected parts should be cut off and discarded.

750g pheasant carcass (backbone discarded) or other game bones and meat

750g pork rib bones

2 tbsp sunflower oil

2 large onions, roughly chopped

1 carrot, roughly chopped

1 stick celery, roughly chopped

1 garlic clove, peeled and sliced in half

2 bay leaves

1 thyme sprig

500ml white wine

special equipment

1–2 roasting tins and a large stockpot

Preheat the oven to 200°C/gas mark 6. Place the bones in a large roasting tin, drizzle with the oil and toss to coat. If you cannot fit the pieces in a single layer use 2 tins. Place in the oven and roast, turning every 20 minutes, until well browned. After 1 hour add the chopped vegetables, garlic and herbs, turning everything occasionally so nothing burns.

After 30 minutes remove from the oven, pour off and discard any fat, and then place the contents of the roasting tin into a stockpot.

Add the wine to the roasting tin or tins and use a wooden spoon to scrape any sediment from the bottom, warming the tins over a low heat to dissolve the juices if necessary, then pour everything from the roasting tins into the stockpot.

Add enough cold water to cover the bones to a depth of 10cm. Bring the stock to a simmer and skim off any fat or scum that rises to the surface. Then turn the heat down to low and leave the stock to simmer very slowly for 6 hours. When cooked, strain the stock through a very fine sieve or chinois into a large bowl, cover and chill.

Once cold, skim any fat from the surface. Pour the stock back into the cleaned stockpot and bring to a boil over a high heat. Reduce to approximately 2 litres, skimming as necessary. Remove the stockpot from the heat and leave to cool. Then chill until cold, pour into re-sealable 250ml containers and freeze for up to 2 months.

To use, thaw out then dilute with an equal quantity of water before using in game soups, braises and casseroles.

DARK CHICKEN STOCK

✳ Makes 1.5 litres ✳ Preparation time 1 hour 15 minutes ✳ Cooking time 6 hours

This full-flavoured chicken stock is made from browned, roasted chicken bones and pieces. It has an intense flavour and light gelatinous body and is excellent with strongly flavoured poultry and game dishes that can stand up to a robust stock.

1.5kg chicken wings and thighs

2 tbsp sunflower oil

1 large carrot, roughly chopped

2 onions, roughly chopped

2 sticks celery, roughly chopped

2 bay leaves

small bunch thyme

special equipment

a roasting tin and a large stockpot

Preheat the oven to 220°C/gas mark 7. Arrange the chicken wings and thighs in a roasting tin and set in the oven. Cook, turning occasionally, for 1 hour, or until the pieces are deep golden-brown in colour.

When the chicken is nearly cooked, place the oil in a large stockpot over medium heat. Add vegetables and fry until lightly coloured. Add the cooked chicken to the pan. Pour off and discard any excess fat in the roasting tin.

Pour a little water into the roasting tin and stir, scraping up any caramelised juices. Pour these into the pan with the vegetables and chicken.

Finally, add the herbs to the chicken and vegetables and pour enough cold water into the stockpot to cover the chicken and vegetables to a depth of 10cm. Turn the heat to high and bring the stock to a simmer, then reduce the heat. Make sure the stock does not boil at any point and skim off any scum that rises to the surface while it is simmering.

After 5 hours, strain the stock through a fine sieve or chinois into a large bowl. Leave it to cool, then cover and chill.

Once it is completely cold, carefully remove any fat from the top. Pour the stock back into the cleaned stockpot, place over a high heat and bring to a boil. Reduce the stock until you are left with 1.5 litres. Remove from the heat to cool, then chill until cold, pour into re-sealable 250ml containers and freeze for up to 2 months. To use, allow the stock to thaw out.

HOLLANDAISE SAUCE

✳ Serves 4 ✳ Preparation time 15 minutes ✳ Cooking time 10 to 15 minutes

Mrs Beeton's Dutch sauce for fish contains a lot less butter than this modern recipe, and a lot more acid (in the original both vinegar and lemon juice are used). Today, we prefer a less sharp sauce, and we commonly serve it not only with fish but also with vegetables such as asparagus, or poured over eggs.

250g unsalted butter

2 large egg yolks

½ tsp lemon juice

salt to taste

special equipment

a heatproof glass or ceramic bowl

Place the butter in a small pan over a medium heat. When it has melted, turn the heat off and keep the pan warm to one side.

Place a heatproof glass or ceramic bowl over a pan of barely simmering water over a low to medium heat. Make sure that the base of the bowl does not touch the water.

Add the egg yolks and lemon juice to the bowl along with ½ tsp water, whisking continuously until they become pale and fluffy. Whisk the hot butter into the egg mixture a little at a time until it is fully incorporated. Continue to whisk until the sauce is thickened and hot. Remove the pan and bowl from the heat to stop it cooking any further and season to taste with a little salt. The sauce can be kept warm over the water for 30 minutes but then must be used, as it will not keep.

SALAD CREAM

✳ Serves 4 ✳ Preparation time 5 minutes ✳ Cooking time 15 minutes

Mrs Beeton gave two cream dressings for salad – delicious sauces that cling to crisp, fresh leaves. They are simillar in fact to the mustardy remoulade sauce used in the French kitchen, but more refined and delicate: perfect when used to dress cos lettuce and radishes. The recipe below is based on one of the originals, with the quantities adjusted slightly to balance the flavours. This quantity will coat approximately 200g of salad leaves.

1 egg

1 tsp mustard

1 large pinch salt

1 large pinch sugar

1 pinch white pepper

1 pinch cayenne pepper

1 tbsp cider or white wine vinegar

6 tbsp single cream

Place the egg in a small pan of cold water and place it on a high heat. Bring to a boil, then reduce the heat to low and cook for 8 minutes. Remove the pan from the heat and lift out the egg with a slotted spoon. Place the egg in a bowl of cold water for five minutes to cool, then peel it and remove the yolk from the white. The white can be reserved for another recipe, or for sprinkling on the salad when ready to eat.

Place the yolk in a medium bowl and mash it with the mustard, salt, sugar, peppers and vinegar until there are no lumps. Slowly stir in the cream, mixing the dressing well to amalgamate. Chill until ready to use. This salad cream will keep for up to 2 days in the fridge.

To use, simply place 200g salad leaves in a large bowl, drizzle over the dressing and toss well. If using, chop the egg white finely and scatter over the salad. Serve immediately.

BÉCHAMEL SAUCE

✳ Makes 500ml ✳ Preparation time 5 minutes ✳ Cooking time 45 minutes including 30 minutes infusing

Béchamel sauce, historically, arose as an amalgam of a stock-based sauce with milk or cream, which is exactly what Mrs Beeton gives in her original recipe. Today, as we are often catering for non-meat eaters, it tends to be made with milk in place of the stock. You can, of course, use half chicken stock and half milk or single cream if you like. Make sure you allow the vegetables and aromatics plenty of time to infuse. For a truly faithful rendition of the original recipe, add a couple of cloves with the bay leaf.

500ml whole milk

½ medium-sized onion, peeled and diced

½ small carrot, peeled and diced

1 tsp black peppercorns

1 fresh bay leaf

35g butter

35g plain flour

salt (optional)

grated nutmeg (optional)

Put the milk, onion, carrot, peppercorns and bay leaf in a saucepan over a medium heat. Bring the mixture to a simmer then remove from the heat. Cover with a lid and leave for 30 minutes to infuse.

When the milk has finished infusing, make a roux. Melt the butter in a small pan over a medium heat. Add the flour and cook for 5 minutes, stirring, until the mixture starts to foam and gives off a delicate toasting aroma. If the flour begins to turn brown or burn at the edges, immediately remove the pan from the heat and dip the base in cold water.

Now bring the milk back to a simmer and strain it through a fine sieve into a large jug, discarding the vegetables. Place the roux back onto a gentle heat and whisk a little of the hot milk into it, blending it in completely before adding a little more. Repeat until all the milk has been added, then continue to simmer the sauce gently for 3–4 minutes until it is glossy, silky and free of lumps. If the sauce tastes floury continue cooking for 1–2 minutes, then season with a little salt and a few gratings of nutmeg, if desired. This sauce can be stored in the fridge, covered closely with cling film, for up to 4 days.

Note: For a simple and tasty cheese sauce, add 80–100g grated Isle of Mull Cheddar and ½ tsp English mustard powder to the hot béchamel sauce, blend well and serve.

PRODUCERS & SUPPLIERS

Spices

Green Saffron Spices

Unit 16, Knockgriffin, Midleton, Cork, Ireland

Tel 00 353 21 463 7960

www.greensaffron.com

Arun and Olive Kapil's family business imports and grinds premium spices from family farms across India.

Meat

Anna's Happy Trotters

Burland, Holme Farm, Howden,
East Yorkshire DN14 7LY

Tel 01430 433030

www.annashappytrotters.com

Delicious and well butchered Yorkshire free-range pork from one of our finest pig farmers, Anna Longthorp.

Graig Farm

Dolau, Llandrindod Wells,
Powys LD1 5TL

Tel 01686 627979

www.graigfarm.co.uk

This farm supplies a wide range of organic products, including meat and poultry, from its online shop. All of their produce is cared for to high standards.

Rhug Estate

Corwen, Denbighshire LL21 0EH

Tel 01490 413000

www.rhug.co.uk

An organic farm and butchery supplying a variety of meat including Aberdeen Angus beef, Salt Marsh lamb, chicken, game and traditional Duroc pork. All the meat (with the exception of the game, which is sourced as locally as possible) is organic and comes from their own farms.

St Brides Farm

High Kype Road, Sandford, Strathaven ML10 6PRT

Tel 01357 529989

www.stbridespoultry.co.uk

Free range chickens and ducks are produced on this small poultry farm just outside of Strathaven, favouring slower growing, flavourful breeds which naturally thrive in the free-range setting.

Cheese and dairy

George Mews Cheese

106 Byres Road,
Glasgow G12 8TB

Tel 0141 334 5900

www.georgemewescheese.co.uk

Specialising in unusual cheeses, George has a carefully balanced selection of world-class British and European artisan cheeses.

Moorlands Cheesemakers

Lorien House, South Street, Castle Cary,
Somerset BA7 7ES

Tel 01963 350634

www.cheesemaking.co.uk

Katrin Loxton sells everything you need to make your own cheeses at home, from various forms of rennet and cultures to complete cheesemaking kits.

Neal's Yard Dairy

108 Druid Street,
London SE1 2HH

Tel 020 7500 7520

www.nealsyarddairy.co.uk

Neal's Yard buy and mature cheese from about seventy cheesemakers on farms around Britain and Ireland. They sell the cheese to shops and restaurants all over the world, and to the public from their two shops in London.

Paxton and Whitfield

93 Jermyn Street,
London SW1Y 6JE

Tel 020 7930 0259

www.paxtonandwhitfield.co.uk

One of the most respected cheesemongers in the country, with a long established history in fine cheese retailing.

PGT Hook & Son

Longleys Farm, Harebeating Lane, Hailsham,
East Sussex BN27 1ER

Tel: 01323 449494

www.hookandson.co.uk

Father and son Phil and Steve Hook farm Longleys
Farm organically and supply extremely natural, pure,
unpasteurised milk, cream and butter from their
sustainably managed cows. They offer a mail order
service from their website.

Herbs and vegetables

Jekka's Herb Farm

Rose Cottage, Shellards Lane, Alveston,
Bristol BS35 3SY

Tel: 01454 418878

www.jekkasherbfarm.com

This award-winning organic herbs nursery sells over 650
varieties of herbs, and hosts open days, workshops and
informative talks on seasonal herbs, throughout the year.

Real Seeds

PO Box 18, Newport near Fishguard,
Pembrokeshire SA65 0AA

Tel: 01239 821107

www.realseeds.co.uk

With a great selection of vegetable seeds on offer, Real
Seeds is a one-stop shop for experienced allotment
owners or absolute beginners. All seeds are chosen
based on what tastes good so don't expect any
flavourless hybrids. Winner of the 'Best Seed Company'
award at the 2011 Horticultre Channel Awards.

The Organic Gardening Catalogue

Riverdene Business Park, Molesey Road, Hersham,
Surrey KT12 4RG

Tel: 01932 253666

www.organiccatalogue.com

A very good range of veg seeds, fruit trees, fertilisers
and composts and plenty of useful organic-gardening-
based sundries.

Useful organisations

FARMA

Lower Ground Floor, 12 Southgate Street,
Winchester, Hampshire SO23 9EF

Tel 0845 45 88 420

www.farmersmarkets.net

The National Farmers' Retail & Markets Association
represents the sale of local food and fresh farm products
direct to the public through farmers' markets and farm
shops. Visit their website for a list of certified markets
and suppliers in your area.

Freedom Food Limited

Wilberforce Way,
Southwater, Horsham,
West Sussex RH13 9RS

Tel 0300 123 0014

www.rspca.org.uk/freedomfood

Freedom Food is the RSPCA's farm assurance and food
labelling scheme. It is the only UK farm assurance
scheme to focus solely on improving the welfare of farm
animals reared for food.

Slow Food UK

Slow Food UK, 6 Neal's Yard,
Covent Garden, London WC2H 9DP

Tel 020 7099 1132

www.slowfood.org.uk

Slow Food UK is part of the global Slow Food movement.
It has thousands of members and connections with local
groups around the UK that link the pleasure of artisan
food to community and the environment.

Soil Association

South Plaza, Marlborough Street,
Bristol BS1 3NX

Tel 0117 314 5000

www.soilassociation.org

The Soil Association is a charity campaigning for
planet-friendly food and farming. It offers guidance to
consumers looking for local suppliers of organic food as
well as advice for organic growers and businesses.

GLOSSARY OF COOKING TERMS

Many languages have influenced the British kitchen, but none so much as French – hardly surprising since French food has often been held up as the benchmark for excellence, in Mrs Beeton's time as well as in our own. Long before the Michelin guide began to report on British restaurants, French chefs were working for British royalty and could be found in the kitchens of many large country houses. Perhaps the most famous of these was Antonin Carême, chef to the Prince Regent (later George IV), who set the standard for future chefs to emulate. Mrs Beeton knew of him by name and reputation. The list below is intended to help explain the more commonly used terms – many, but not all, of which come from the French.

al dente   a term used to describe foods such as pasta, rice and vegetables that are cooked but still have a firmness to the bite

au gratin   describes a cooked dish topped with a browned crust, usually made by finishing with grated cheese or breadcrumbs and browning under the grill

bisque   a shellfish stock or soup, often with added cream

blanch   to boil briefly, often in order to loosen the skin from nuts and kernels, to part-cook green vegetables or to remove strong or bitter flavours

blend   to combine ingredients to give a smooth mixture

braise   to cook slowly in a covered pan or dish, with liquid

brown   to colour the surface of a food by cooking it in hot fat, caramelising the sugars and developing flavour

casserole   a deep, lidded cooking pot made from an ovenproof material

chill   to cool food without freezing, usually in a refrigerator

chinois   a conical sieve with a very fine mesh used for straining soups, sauces and purées to give a very smooth result

clarify   (of stock) to remove sediment or filter using egg white

cocotte   a small dish in which eggs, mousses and soufflés are baked

colander   a metal or plastic basket used for draining food such as cooked vegetables

de-glaze   to add liquid to a pan after roasting or sautéeing in order to dissolve any juices or sediment left in the base of the pan, picking up their flavour

dice   to cut food into small cubes

flambé or flame   to remove the alcohol from hot food by lighting the fumes

fold in   to combine ingredients carefully with a whisk, metal spoon or spatula in order to retain any air that has been incorporated into the mixutre

gelatine   a setting agent derived from the bones of animals, used for setting jellies

glaze   a glossy finish given to food, usually by brushing with beaten egg or milk before cooking, or with sugar syrup after cooking

infuse   to combine aromatic herbs and/or vegetables with a liquid such as stock or milk (or, in the case of tea making, water) and leave them for a period of time to impart their flavour

jelly   a liquid set with gelatine or another gelling agent

legumes   podded vegetables such as peas, beans and lentils

liaison   a thickening or binding agent, for example a roux, arrowroot mixture, egg yolk or cream

macedoine   a mixture of various kinds of vegetables or fruits cut into small dice

maître d'hôtel   cooked and/or served with parsley

mirepoix   a mixture of finely chopped vegetables, usually onion, carrot and celery

ovenproof   describes cookware or crockery that can be used in the oven

par-boil   to part cook in water

poach   to cook food in simmering liquid

purée   food that has been blended or passed through a sieve to give a smooth texture

ramekin   a small ceramic, ovenproof dish, often used for soufflés or creams

reduce   to concentrate a liquid, for example a sauce or stock, by boiling it until a portion has evaporated

roast   to cook in the oven or on a spit over an open flame

roux   a mixture made from equal quantities of fat and flour cooked together and used as a thickening agent for sauces

sauté   to fry food in hot shallow fat, turning it frquently, until it is evenly browned

score   to cut shallow gashes into the surface of food before cooking

sear   to brown meat rapidly using a fierce heat to seal in the juices

seasoned flour   flour mixed with salt and pepper, and sometimes other spices, often used to coat meat or fish before cooking

season   to add salt, pepper, spices, herbs or other ingredients to food to add flavour or (at the end of the cooking time) to correct the balance of flavours

sift   to pass flour or sugar through a sieve to remove any lumps and/or incorporate air

skim   to remove residue from the surface of a liquid, for example fat from stock or scum from jam

soufflé   a baked dish consisting of a sauce or purée, usually thickened with egg yolks and lightened with beaten egg whites, which rises during cooking

steep   to soak in liquid, in order to hydrate

stew   to simmer food slowly in a casserole or covered pan

stockpot   a large, deep pan for making stock

sweat   to gently soften chopped vegetables in hot oil or butter

vinaigrette   a dressing for salad or vegetables, made with a base of oil and vinegar

zest   the coloured outer skin of citrus fruits in which the highly flavoured oils are contained

INDEX

ACKNOWLEDGEMENTS

Mum, Sandra Baker, helped without question in the kitchen and office both in the process of testing the recipes and in organising manuscripts – you are a blessing.

To my sister Louise, and to Oscar and Fanny for providing moral support go hearty thanks. Much respect and love goes to Dad, John Baker, whose vegetable garden is without parallel.

Joyce Molyneux, my great friend and mentor, celebrated seasonal and local food years before it was trendy and taught me to respect nuance, delicacy and care in her kitchen – thankyou. Thanks also to Adam Sellar, who provided great support in the kitchen during the testing of these recipes.

Amanda Harris and Debbie Woska sat through the creation of *Mrs Beeton How to Cook* with me – providing just the right amount of support and encouragement – thank you.

Zelda Turner deserves thanks for helping trim and sculpt the recipes in this smaller collection. To all the design team – Julyan Bayes, Lucie Steriker, Sammy-Jo Squire and her crew, and the photographer Andrew Hayes-Watkins and his team for making the book look so beautiful. The team behind the scenes at Orion helped enormously – Elizabeth Allen and Nicky Carswell especially.

George Ward and crew at Fresh and Fruity in Hedon deserve many thanks for always having a smile and providing me with superb fruit and veg, season by season.

Finally, thanks to Alice Waters and Joy Larkcom who always manage to inspire and teach.

Gerard Baker